Mom Thanks To You Notebook
Best Mom Ever Lined Journal – Gifts for Mom
Paperback ISBN: 978-1-989733-15-8
Published by Dunhill Clare Publishing 2020
 Cover Design by Sharon Purtill

www.ingramcontent.com/pod-product-compliance
Lightning Source LLC
Chambersburg PA
CBHW070515200726
48293CB00007B/2557

* 9 7 8 1 9 8 9 7 3 3 1 5 8 *